Tsim T

BY
L. ST MARS.

NEW YORK,
PUBLISHED BY W. HALL & SON, 229 BROADWAY.

Sabrina Orah Mark

saturnalia books

Saturnalia Books
105 Woodside Rd.
Ardmore, PA 19003
info@saturnaliabooks.com

ISBN: 978-0-9818591-2-5
Library of Congress Control Number: 2009930090

Book Design by Saturnalia Books
Printing by Westcan Printing Group, Canada

Cover Art: *The Hippopotamus Polka*
courtesy of Keffer Collection of Sheet Music, University of Pennsylvania Library

Distributed by:
University Press of New England
1 Court Street
Lebanon, NH 03766
800-421-1561

Grateful acknowledgment is made to the editors of the following publications in which these poems first appeared, occasionally as reprints or in slightly altered form:

Action, Yes: "All Is Fair in Love and War"
The Believer: "B Is for Beatrice"
The Best American Poetry 2007: "The 10 Stages of Beatrice"
Black Clock: "The Delivery," "The Departure," "The Disasters," "Long Ago and Far Away," "The Organization"
Black Warrior Review: "Where Babies Come From," "Birthday"
Boston Review: "The Drawing"
Columbia Poetry Review: "Aster," "Cryptozoology"
Conduit: "The 10 Stages of Beatrice," "The Description," "Poland," "The Joke," "Forgiveness"
Cranky: "The Oldest Animal Writes a Letter Home," "On the Way to Mist Must"
Fishouse: "The Box," "The Name," "The Reality Testing Booth," "The Saddest Gown in the World," "Walter B.'s Extraordinary Cousin Arrives for a Visit"
Forklift, Ohio: "The Creation," "The Stethoscope"
Harvard Review: "The Ruse," "The Word"
The Indiana Review: "The Reality Testing Booth"
Jubilat: "The Definition of a Thief," "The Healer"
Octopus Magazine: "The Marks of Walter B.'s Power," "Parashas Acharei Mos," "The Traitor"
Soft Targets: "The History of Stray," "The Preservation"
Typo: "Beatrice Takes a Lover," "Walter B. Needs Some Time," "The Mistake"

Some of the poems in this book were published in 2006 by Woodland Editions as a chapbook entitled *Walter B.'s Extraordinary Cousin Arrives for a Visit & Other Tales.*

Thanks: Harriet Bass, Oni Buchanan, Judith Ortiz Cofer, Andrew Cole, Brian Connell, Amber Dermont, Michael Dumanis, Jane Elias, Ronnie Gorden, Zachary Gorden, Beatrice Hanssen, Kristen Iskandrian, Henry Israeli, Kirsten Kaschock, Brielle Mark, Danielle Mark, Eve McKnight, Moriah McKnight, Rachael McKnight, Ed Pavlic, Claudia Rankine, Jed Rasula, Matthew Shindell, Brian Teare, John Woods, Jay Worenklein, Sasha Worenklein, & Foryst. To Lucy, who will always be T.O.A. To the Mark, Malitzky, & Sternklar families—especially Jack & Lila Sternklar. To Gertrude Mark, my partner in crime. To Eugene Mark, above & beyond. To Etan Mark & Ari Mark—my water & my air. To my mother for strength. To my father for wonder.

The writing of this book was made possible in part through the generous support of the University of Georgia, & a Literature Fellowship from the National Endowment for the Arts.

This might seem difficult to believe, but I was such a human being once. I had a kind of feeling living among Walter B.

—*Beatrice* (from "The Walter B. Interviews")

TABLE OF CONTENTS

for Reginald McKnight, my tsim & my tsum

I

say goodbye – a banquet – the last bite of fish – the timbrelist –
the thief – an egg filled with red sugar – disasters – goat song – a booth –
between worlds

The Departure

"You do not know anymore," sighed Walter B., "what is real." "Goodbye," said Beatrice. "Goodbye," said Walter B. "Goodbye," said Beatrice. "Goodbye," said Walter B. "Where will you go?" asked Beatrice. "To the banquet," said Walter B. Beatrice stared at him. She wished he would break like the sky once did and drown her in flowers. "Weren't we once," asked Beatrice softly, "a little like a banquet?" "You do not know anymore," sighed Walter B., "what is real." Walter B. and Beatrice stood in the dark. They held hands and watched the wagons pass by. Walter B. was not in any of them. "Goodbye," said Beatrice. "Goodbye," said Walter B. "Goodbye," said Beatrice. "Goodbye," said Walter B. "Where will you go?" asked Beatrice. "To the banquet," said Walter B. Behind them the horses were slowly gathering in the frozen field. "Weren't we once," asked Beatrice softly, "a little like a banquet?" "You do not know anymore," sighed Walter B., "what is real." "Goodbye," said Beatrice. "Goodbye," said Walter B. "Goodbye," said Beatrice. "Goodbye," said Walter B. "Where will you go?" asked Beatrice. "To the banquet," said Walter B. Walter B. and Beatrice stood in the dark. They held hands and watched the wagons pass by. Walter B. was not in any of them. "Goodbye," said Beatrice. "Goodbye," said Walter B. "Goodbye," said Beatrice. "Goodbye," said Walter B.

Walter B. Needs Some Time

When Walter B., one evening, explained to Beatrice that he "needed time," Beatrice pulled the last bite of fish from Walter B.'s mouth and shook it at him. She wished he had said instead that he needed a timbrel, and off they would have gone together to the spectacle where the timbrelist often played. But Walter B. did not need a timbrel. Walter B. "needed time." So Beatrice wrapped what was left of the fish in a red wool cloth and set out to find him some. It was cold outside. If I was time, wondered Beatrice, where would I be? She watched the humans in the distance breathe into the grass. If I was time, wondered Beatrice, how would I remind myself of where I was? She held the last bite of fish up to her mouth for warmth. It began to feel heavy in her hands. She wished he had said instead that he needed a timbrel. She wished she was for Walter B. the time he needed. But she was not. She unwrapped the last bite of fish and studied it. It reminded her of a world inside of which Walter B. was mostly gone. She rubbed her arms with it. She buried her face in it. It began to grow around her like a soft, white house. It grew, and it grew, until at last Beatrice was inside. She slowly walked through its rooms. In the first room, a pile of shovels. In the second, a pitcher of milk. When she stepped inside the third, Walter B. and the timbrelist were helping each other on with their coats. "If you were time," called out Walter B., "where would you be?" Before Beatrice could answer, Walter B. saluted her, took the timbrelist by the hand, and left her alone in the soft, white house. Beatrice sat on the floor. Much later she would drink from the pitcher of milk. She would lean against the pile of shovels. But for now all Beatrice could do was sit on the floor. She would sit on the floor of the soft, white house until she grew hungry again for Walter B.'s last bite of fish.

The Definition of a Thief

Walter B., as he rummaged through Beatrice's blouse pockets, asked her carefully what the word "thief" meant. He had heard this word before. Once in the great field. And once in the kitchen. It felt like a word with great distance. For years it had already seemed too late to ask. But not with Beatrice. Not now. With Beatrice he could ask anything. Gently removing his hands, as he had once removed hers, Beatrice said, "it is an instance, Walter B., of carrying away something that is not yours to carry away. For example," she continued, "if I am carried away by an idea, this idea becomes for me a thief. I become nothing, in this instance, but a stolen object. I comb my hair and eat my breakfast only in the realm of this idea. To be a thief, Walter B., and this is the most important part, to be a thief means to be a person who is only able to be an existing idea if he or she carries away and then dwells in another. Do you understand?" she asked. But Walter B. had stopped listening. He was staring at Beatrice's mouth. As if he could reach inside it and pull out a long gray hair. Or an egg filled with red sugar.

The Disasters

Beatrice decided it was time to commodify her disasters. She spread each one out on the floor and studied them. Some would open. Some would not. Outside, the humans sailed past each other like thin discarded boats. Beatrice lifted each disaster up to the light. The rustle of a faraway fairground hung in the air. "If only," thought Beatrice, "I could make from one of these a profit I would be saved." Some chirped happily. Some were in no mood to be touched. Walter B. listened from the other room. "What are you doing in there, my little shipwreck?" "Commodifying my disasters," said Beatrice. "That's nice," said Walter B. "Will you need some batteries?" "No," said Beatrice. "Better save the batteries for the children." The Collector arrived at the door. Walter B. sent him away. Beatrice counted her disasters. 174. They were all accustomed to the best of care. "If only," thought Beatrice, "I had a cart." But she did not have a cart. "Not since Poland," Walter B. reminded her. "If only," thought Beatrice, "I had a kiosk." But she did not have a kiosk either. Beatrice sat with her disasters all evening. "How can I wrap these beautiful creatures in paper," Beatrice wondered, "and send them off for a price?" Beatrice felt disheveled. The Collector arrived at the door. Walter B. sent him away. From far off, Beatrice could hear the humans getting tangled in their blankets. Walter B. cautiously stepped over Beatrice's disasters. "I regret," he said, "your desire to commodify." He pulled Beatrice onto his lap. "For one," he continued, looking around, "this may be our only hope for a family. And for second, look how closely they resemble us." Some yawned. Some bristled with difficulty. Others were telling stories about their times in the woods. Beatrice looked around. She knew she would have to keep them. Walter B. rocked Beatrice gently. He kissed her in the middle of her sleepy face. "It really is astonishing," said Walter B., overflowing with pride, "what you with all my love have made." Some were crawling into their bed. Others had already begun to sing The Goat Song.

The Reality Testing Booth

At the Reality Testing Booth, or as Beatrice liked to say, "at the Reality Testing Boof," Beatrice and Walter B. had a realization. It was almost morning. They brought with them four things to test: hat, love, day, and the delectable. Each test required a small gold token. They were a little scared. Walter B. only had enough for three, and Beatrice, well Beatrice, she was all out of small gold tokens. It was strange to choose, but it seemed only right to first test an object, so they held the hat up first and waited for the printout. They waited for a long time. They waited for hours. And then they waited for days. It was a long, long wait, this waiting. Walter B. began, in this waiting, to speak of "the objective evaluation of situations that enable one to distinguish between the external and internal worlds and between the self and the nonself." Beatrice listened. She listened carefully, and as she listened she began to grow very fond of Walter B. As if it was actually he who was the love that made each of her days delectable.

II

debacle – twirled and twirled – these babies were not the same babies –
door slam – very far away – at the assembly – whoop and holler –
fork or a spoon – the horse – good luck – revenge – forgive

Beatrice Takes a Lover

"I am taking a lover," Beatrice announced, flipping through the phone book procreatively. "And where exactly," asked Walter B., fussing with his fur collar, "will you be taking this lover?" "To the debacle, Walter B." Walter B. was miffed. "You are being, Beatrice, neither relevant nor sensible." Beatrice felt warned. She felt like she should cook for Walter B. some soup tonight in fairly graphic detail. "Why," asked Walter B., brushing the fur off his neck, "to the debacle?" Beatrice thought for a moment. She considered the beauty of Walter B.'s ruin. "Because I want," said Beatrice, "some astonishment." "What in god's name," asked Walter B., "is wanting some astonishment?" Beatrice began to worry she had read the wrong book. She went into the yard, which she often did when she felt unsure. Walter B. followed. "Astonishment, Walter B.," continued Beatrice, staring at the ground, "is when you take a lover to the debacle." "I see," said Walter B. He began to reconsider his position. He knew somewhere deep in Beatrice's heart that this was not terrific. He knew that this was very, very far from terrific. He wanted very much to unbutton her blouse. He wanted to touch her thighs in a way neither Beatrice nor Walter B. would later remember. "And furthermore, Walter B.," Beatrice continued, "I have been feeling, lately, like a scene of simplicity." "But why not take a lover," asked Walter B., "to a field or to a bridge or to Mother's? Why," he moaned, "to the debacle?" "Because of god," said Beatrice. Walter B. could hardly believe his ears. He could hardly believe this wonderful turn of events. Beatrice would take a lover to the debacle because of god! "You have made me, sweet Beatrice, very, very happy. Happier, in fact, than I have ever been in my entire life. So happy, in fact, that I would like to twirl." "So twirl," said Beatrice, feeling, at last, very pleased with herself. And so Walter B. twirled. He twirled, and he twirled, and he twirled. He twirled until there was no twirling left in the whole wide world.

Where Babies Come From

"Where," asked Beatrice, "do babies come from?" Walter B. was hanging a painting in the crawl space. It was a painting of the babies. "Basically," said Walter B., "babies come from rubbing babies together. They rub and they rub. Once, I heard them rubbing." "Are you sure those are the babies where babies come from?" asked Beatrice. She was staring at the painting. It was a painting of the babies. Walter B. stepped back. "They seem," said Beatrice, "to be different babies." Walter B. tilted his head. A door slammed. They stood for a long time and examined the painting. Beatrice was right. These were not the same babies. These were different babies. Some of these babies carried twine. These were not the babies where babies came from. Some of these babies were not rubbing. Some of these babies had books about babies tucked under their arms. These were not the same babies. These babies would never be the babies where babies came from. These babies were different. And Beatrice was the first to call their bluff.

Aster

According to Walter B., an "aster" denotes "something that imperfectly resembles or mimics the true thing." When he says this he is alphabetizing the appliances: Beater, Coffee Maker, Mixer, Spatula, Toaster. Beatrice reminds him, from between the beater and the coffee maker, that "aster" is also a combining form with the meaning "star." Sometimes these reminders seem very, very far away. Does this mean, wonders Walter B. distantly, that there is only to resemble "the true thing"? That there is only to be reminded of the star from between what once seemed like a beautiful assemblage of order? "No," says Beatrice, brushing the feathers off his dear, dear head. Beatrice likes to think of herself in all of Walter B.'s disastrous places.

The Marks of Walter B.'s Power

At the assembly, Walter B. listed for Beatrice the marks of his power. "One," he began, "'delight,' two 'refusal,' three 'blockage,' four 'the momentous event'…" "The momentous event?" interrupted Beatrice. "Yes," said Walter B., "the momentous event." Walter B. turned the page. "Now," he asked, "where was I?" "You were," said Beatrice, "at the momentous event." The humans began to file into the auditorium. Walter B. waited for them to take their seats and then he continued. "Five 'imminence,' six 'surrender'…" At "surrender" there was a whoop from the back of the room, and then there was a holler. Walter B. blushed and then he continued. "Seven 'possession'…" "For this momentous event," interrupted Beatrice, "there was a broadcast?" Walter B. was not getting out of Beatrice's interruptions a kick. "Owing to the intimate nature of the momentous event," sighed Walter B., "there was no broadcast." "Not even a flier?" asked Beatrice. "No," said Walter B., "not even a flier." Weeping filled the room. It was becoming too clear to Walter B. that Beatrice had forgotten how to listen to his litany without deep feelings of exclusion. Nevertheless, he continued. "Eight 'enchantment,' nine 'evasion'…" "Not even," asked Beatrice, "a hint? Not even a clue?" The humans threw their heads back and closed their eyes. Walter B. turned his notes over and stared at Beatrice. "What would you like," asked Walter B., "for me to tell you? That it was a night of eternal bliss and fear?" "That would be nice," said Beatrice, "for starters." "Fine," said Walter B. "It was a night of eternal bliss and fear." Beatrice gasped. She began to tremble with disgrace. The humans began to quickly file out of the auditorium. They swore never to speak of the assembly again, and they swore to forgive each other for what they now knew. They swore to look away when they would, years later, come across Beatrice in her yard with her spools, and her lights, and her dust, trying to build for Walter B. the exact momentous event he once attended without her. And although they knew not to watch Beatrice as she measured and sawed, they often thought back to that day at the assembly and wondered, hopelessly, if the tenth mark of Walter B.'s power was Beatrice.

Forgiveness

Walter B. had an idea. He would arrive at the door in a white linen suit with scarlet cuffs and beg for Beatrice's forgiveness. Should he bring for her a fork or a spoon? He could not decide. He would ask the horse.

The horse thought the spoon. But the spoon, the spoon would remind her of the pudding. And the pudding would remind her of the babies. And the babies (the horse did not yet know this) would remind Beatrice of the baking sheet she held above her head as she ran, and ran, and ran far into the city. He should have, like the babies, run along beside her. But the horse thought the spoon. Walter B.'s hands stiffened. Beatrice would be back any minute. He removed the fork and the spoon from the pocket of his white linen suit and shook them for good luck. One for now, he decided. And one for later. He began to feel brave. Should he beg for Beatrice's forgiveness, he wondered, or should he take on her revenge? He could not decide. He would ask the horse.

The horse thought revenge. But revenge (the horse did not yet know this) would remind Beatrice of forgiveness...

III

soldiers dressed like children – candy – a large black bird – prayer –
they once were beautiful – Poland – an illustrated book –
sliced apples – the suspicion of the town

The Traitor

A few days before the first snow the soldiers dressed like children began to appear. "Come quick," said Beatrice, fetching Walter B. away from his scripture, "and bring candy!" Walter B. pulled on his robe and joined Beatrice on the balcony. "Oh look," said Beatrice, "you can see their small, sweet eyes peeking through the bramble." Walter B. threw a handful of red gumdrops into the air and watched the soldiers dressed like children scatter, and raise their arms in glee. "Feels sinful, doesn't it?" purred Beatrice. They watched them stand in the field and chew. "Which one," asked Walter B., "do you think is the hero?" "That one," said Beatrice. "Definitely that one. The one with the mittens." "Yes," agreed Walter B., "the others seem less… festooned." "And which one do you think," asked Walter B., "is the traitor?" Beatrice bit her lip and looked around. "Maybe that one," she said. "The one with the orange flower in the pocket of his vest." Walter B. agreed, but to be certain he thought that he should ask. "Little traitor," called out Walter B. The traitor looked up. "I knew it!" said Beatrice, clapping her hands. The traitor came closer. The wind shook the orange flower loose from his pocket, but he did not run after it. He missed his mother. The traitor came closer, but then he stopped. He curled into his flowerless vest and fell asleep. Walter B. and Beatrice yawned. The soldiers dressed like children opened their mouths as wide as they could, but there was no more candy. There would never again be more candy. And so they sailed away to another land.

Cryptozoology

Like many translated biological terms, "Beatrice" lacks the connotative impact of its foreign original. Essentially an ideological term, "Beatrice" refers to a small, poorly lit room where paintings of Beatrice are haphazardly displayed. When Beatrice explained this to Walter B. one night, without warning, Walter B. was so relieved he slept in his boots. It was as if this secret Beatrice no longer kept lifted from Walter B.'s arms a large black bird as heavy as Beatrice. "Many of the paintings," continued Beatrice, "suggest scenes of yard play gone awry. Like this one over here," she said, pointing to one where a rake is nestled lovingly against her cheek. "Other paintings depict me as frothy," she continued. "Like that one," she said, spinning around the small room as if it were a room she once owned. "See how frothy I am, Walter B., and how confidently I clutch a smaller Beatrice." Why exactly the smaller Beatrice Beatrice clutched wore lipstick and dark knee socks, and why there was a barren tree nearby, Walter B. was too excited to ask. If Walter B. could have climbed inside that painting and slept against the two Beatrices, forever, he would have.

Beatrice Writes a Letter to a Magazine

"Dear Magazine, in your last issue you list the 50 most beautiful, but how could you forget the cellar door, the Walter B., one year before his death the clawfoot tub, the ruse, the green balloon, to sing The Goat Song is very beautiful. Dear Magazine, the harvest, too. To say a word is beautiful. In your last issue you forget I knelt beside the sandwich cart and prayed. Was it deliberate you left the babies out, or by mistake? The booth, the signup sheet, the woods are all so goddamn beautiful and you forget. And I forget out of which banquet did you stumble from, dear Magazine. You forget how beautiful the banquet was."

Beatrice looked up from her letter. She studied the notes Walter B. prepared for her. She applied to her lips the ointment, and continued:

"Dear Magazine, and also you forget herself. For example, last night I bit into a nuptial. It had a cherry filling. I licked the sides and threw the wrapper out. You forget how beautiful the wrapper was. And you forget I once and am still now inside the house where all the animals are neatly tagged. They are so neatly tagged. They once were beautiful, too. We beg for a correction. You forget how beautifully we beg."

Poland

Beatrice used for the first time today the word "Poland." As in, "Walter B., we are not in Poland." As soon as Beatrice used the word once, she could not for the life of her stop. Not, at least, with Walter B. standing like that with his mouth open. She did not know, at first, if saying the word like she did was a doom or a place to kneel. As in, "Hold me here while I am still not in Poland." Historically, she could not say it to Walter B. enough. Even when Beatrice saw that Walter B. had begun to feel harmed by the word, she curled up very small on the sofa and whispered into her knees, "Take, for me, the babies back to Poland." She was beginning, by now, to feel beside herself. Something on Walter B.'s face began to look as though he had had enough. But of what he had had enough, Beatrice pretended not to know. "Poland?" she asked. "Have you had enough of Poland?" They were beginning, very quickly, not to understand each other. They were beginning to feel as though they were in Poland. Not like lovers, as they had once, in Poland, hoped to be, but like children wearing very, very bright colors. Two children pulling, like horses, a cart. They began to feel as though something very small and very alive was among them in this cart. "Something...like Poland?" Beatrice asked. Walter B., by now, was furious. He decided, once and for all, to see what very small and very alive thing was among them. He left Beatrice alone to hold up the cart, while he went to see for himself the thing that had come between them. The thing they were, like horses, pulling. Beatrice began to feel very beautiful and very real holding the cart up by herself as she did. A few minutes later Walter B. returned with a thin layer of sawdust covering his lips. "Was it Poland?" Beatrice asked. "No," said Walter B., slowly disappearing. "It never really was."

The Town

It was time, decided Walter B., to make out of Beatrice a secret. He would need a town. He would need for this town a population. He felt someone watching him. If it is the population watching me, thought Walter B., I'm well on my way. If it is Beatrice, remembered Walter B., she is of no concern. He put on the hood, squinted, and waved. "We're so lucky," one of them said. Walter B. looked at the instructions. First, he should tie to Beatrice's trousers a long rope, and to the rope he should tie a message: "to whom," it should read, "belongs this." He couldn't think to shoot her. It is similar with hawks and babies, but it is even more similar with Beatrice. No one ever thinks to shoot her. "I love," whispered Beatrice, "the government archives." And she was not the only one. "Shhh…" warned Walter B. Beatrice began to feel discreet. She began to walk with a stoop not like a thief, but like a thief in an illustrated book of thieves. "Now," said Walter B., "we're getting somewhere." And somewhere they were getting. "There are so few of us here," said Beatrice, surveying the town. And where they were getting Beatrice was scarce. Walter B. rejoiced. He prepared for Beatrice a plate of beef apples. He sliced them cautiously so as not to arouse the suspicion of the town.

IV

*if it occurs in winter it is called "The Babies" – gifts –
ecstasy – the ninth stage – delivery – where organs come from –
a mistake – a field – nurses – mice – laughter*

The 10 Stages of Beatrice

Stage 1. — Belonging.

In the first stage Beatrice is precisely labeled and timed. She is able to devise complex graphs, answer questions in the order that they're asked, and construct coherent narratives without nostalgia or actual fear. There is no display of loud sobbing, nor are there visions.

Stage 2. — Happy.

Beatrice, during the second stage, believes she is alive. The possibility that she is not alive, in this stage, never enters her mind. This stage is only possible if the spectacle comes to town.

Stage 3. — Walter B.

This stage is also called "the latch stage." It is Beatrice at her most historical and strange.

Stage 4. — Romance.

Beatrice is hunted, captured, and softly strung to a tree. In this stage words are used to intoxicate, supply, and deceive. These words are rarely interesting. Gifts are exchanged that are of no use.

Stage 5. — Dread.

Beatrice is covered in feathers and twigs. She believes she is a nest. This stage, if it occurs in winter, is also called "The Babies."

Stage 6. — Slice.

The sixth stage often appears in Beatrice's hand like a long instrument with a blade at the end. She will eat cake, during this stage, until she has visions.

Stage 7. — Cryptozoology.

In the seventh stage Beatrice wears a green dress with large white pockets in which to store the evidence. If this stage is mingled with the second stage, ecstasy is achieved.

Stage 8. — Crowded.

Beatrice is behind glass. In this stage Beatrice is blurred by the humans who observe her without caution.

Stage 9. — Poland.

Beatrice gathers her grandfather into her arms. She recites him from his memory. The ninth stage sounds like this: tsim tsum, tsim tsum, tsim tsum.

Stage 10. — Return.

In the final stage Beatrice watches Beatrice feed the babies with a spade.

The Delivery

In our pressed brown suit we deliver the document to Beatrice and Walter B. The document glows in our hand. We take three steps and we are where they are cutting up smocks. For luck, we figure. He is up to her knees in rust and mink. She is up to his knees, as per his instructions. If we could fold the document up inside her pale mouth. If we could remove the black canister from her arms. If we were kind we would. He holds her up to the light. "Reminds you of a pharmacy, doesn't she?" And she does. She reminds us of a pharmacy.

The Organization

"If we ever want to know, Walter B., where our organs have come from, we will have to join the organization." Beatrice explains this to Walter B. as she climbs down from where he had once held her to the light. "For too long, Walter B., we have believed our organs have come to us from the forest, and I am beginning to fear they have not." Walter B. tried very hard to remember. Had their organs arrived with the scent of mud or insects or leaves? Or had they arrived from somewhere else? He once read that some organs arrive sweet and wiry, while others arrive dark and soft. He could not remember how their organs had arrived. They would have to join the organization. The recently delivered document asked that they sign their names at the bottom. They would have to conform to the standards, rules, and demands of the organization if they ever wanted to know from where their organs had come. In an instance like this, Walter B. believed that Beatrice knew what was best. According to the document, they would have to empty their house of their oldest animal. They would have to brush their doorpost with its leftover fur. "It is a sorrowful thing to join an organization," explained Beatrice as she led their oldest animal out from where it had been kept so long. "But it must, I am afraid, be done." Walter B. nodded. Beatrice blushed. And why exactly she blushed, Walter B. would not find out until later that evening.

The Mistake

A mistake had been made. "Should we shoot it?" asked Walter B. "Of course," sighed Beatrice, "we should not shoot it." It stood in the long grass and blinked at them. "Where do you think," asked Beatrice, "it came from." "From the debacle, I suppose," is all Walter B. said. And then he considered, "Or maybe from the babies." Beatrice tugged at her sleeves. A mistake had been made, and now Walter B. and Beatrice had on their hands a situation. "How," asked Walter B., "do you suppose such a mistake had been made?" The mistake began to pose, as if it heard him. It staggered across the field. For a moment it looked like a woman bent over nothing in particular. And then it rose. And then it opened its mouth. "Oh, look," exclaimed Beatrice, "it's communicating!" "Is it alone?" whispered Walter B., taking Beatrice's hand. "Yes," Beatrice whispered back, "I think it is alone." But it was not alone. It was not alone at all. Others began to emerge. Some from the trees. Some from the grass. Their damp white mouths flashed in the sunlight. "Had I known a little ahead of time," said Walter B., "I would have changed into my suit." "Yes," agreed Beatrice, "we should have arrived more prepared." "This is exactly what," said Walter B., raising his voice and pointing at the scene in front of them, "I had been trying to explain to you. And now we are in a situation without any rope." "Pardon me," said Beatrice. And she began to walk into the field. Slowly, at first. And then faster. And then she began to run. She ran with her arms outstretched, as one might run into a field filled with mothers.

The Joke

What didn't kill Beatrice that winter made her funnier. She was wounded, yes, but she was funnier. Victory was hers. She hobbled home, past the wagons climbing with nurses. Past the beautiful trees. "Ah," cried Walter B., "my voluptuous goat has returned from battle! My sugar packet is back from the front!" He waved an empty flag. "Sit, sit," said Walter B. "I'll garnish a roast." Beatrice opened with an old joke. She was like a riot. Walter B. beamed. He laughed and he laughed. Her wounds were startling, but her jokes were transcendent. She tore her gunnysack open for a tender punchline. A dirty punchline. A punchline to end all punchlines, as the soldiers say. Walter B. turned the oven on high and guffawed. It was a hot afternoon. Too sunny to tell one nurse from another. But the nurses were there. Oh, they were there. They huddled at the window. Hundreds of them. Maybe thousands. They scratched at the door. Someone should have let them in. But who? Who could hear them above all that laughter? They were sweating now. Gleaming. They scrambled over each other like mice. They were pounding. Thumping. Thumping nurses. Beatrice had just begun a new joke when she noticed one had gotten in. A large one. A large nurse. A large laughing nurse. But why was she laughing? Even Walter B. knew it was too soon to tell how this joke would end.

V

On the Way to Mist Must

"Where are we?" asked Beatrice. "We are very close," said Walter B. They stared steadily ahead. "Where is very close?" asked Beatrice. "It is right before," said Walter B., "we get there." Beatrice's imagination zoomed past them in a white fur coat. "There it goes again," sighed Beatrice, "running wild." It somersaulted twice, then charged into the distance. "Get back here," hollered Walter B. He wrung his hands. He stomped his feet. "I'd like to give that good-for-nothing a piece of my mind," he grumbled. But Beatrice's imagination was running wild. It hurtled back and stared Walter B. in the face. It mocked a yawn. "You are a hopeless little thing!" cursed Walter B. Beatrice's imagination stopped. It looked cautiously around as if it knew something about the world the world would never know. Then it bounded away. "Should we catch up?" asked Beatrice, buttoning her sweater. "We should not," warned Walter B., "catch up." "Where are we?" asked Beatrice. "We are very close," said Walter B. "Where is very close?" asked Beatrice. "It is right before," said Walter B., "we get there." The sign up the road read "Mist Must." Beatrice's imagination leaned against the sign and nibbled on a large cashew. "Oh goody," clapped Beatrice. "It's already there. And with provisions!" Walter B. trembled. For years he was brave enough to come this close. Wasn't that enough, he wondered. Maybe it was for Beatrice. Maybe it was, he muttered to himself, until her imagination showed up in a white fur coat with a cashew large enough for everyone.

The Preservation

"What is this thing," asked Beatrice, "to overfloweth?" It was late August. Walter B. and Beatrice were reading from The Collector's Cautionary Tale when to Beatrice this question occurred. "To overfloweth, Beatrice," explained Walter B. in a hatched voice neither Walter B. nor Beatrice had ever heard before, "is to deposit too much life into either the babies or Poland." Beatrice thought for a moment. She thought about The Collector. She thought about his grammar. She thought about caution. She wanted very much to overfloweth. "How, specifically," asked Beatrice, motioning in The Collector, who had gathered by the door to listen, "does a human overfloweth?" Walter B. began to think about preservation. He thought if only he could apply it, like earth, to her body. If only The Collector had not brought with him an answer, he could keep Beatrice from depositing too much life. Too much life, he had decided years ago, should not by Beatrice ever be deposited.

The Oldest Animal Writes a Letter Home

To That Mutter and That Fodder:

It is of the upmostly imports that I wrotted you concerping the whereaboutlings of That Mutter"'s amangination. I seep it daily runnING to and froth. Something is wrong wif it? Why does it says a revolupshun is in order as it rubs its teeers away wif the grasses? Was it That Mutter who is alpso called Be Trice who hath given it the witfir coat it sheds all over the Foryst and the Skyys? That same Mutter who hath given me all the outside parts of the whirld? On a certain evening when I was scayred, That Mutter"'s amangination really brought me the herrings and the marmalades. We ated all of it ups under the moops and the starps. In de mouf the herrings and the marmalades taysted like wyrds scraped auf the bones of That Mutter if she is misting me. That Mutter"'s A. laffed, and laffed, when I said that idear out lord. That Mutter"'s A. laffed so open I could seep into its mouf all the way down to the inside of its feats. A gastling wynd shakes from there. Even I (The Oldest Animal) can hear the ghastling wynd sayeth all my thinks at once. Remember when That Fodder who is alpso called Double You Be said That Mutter"'s A. should stand in the corner and think about what it did? What does it do? Nuffing, mostling. Except for all the wynds. And the herrings. And the marmalades. Hencefroth and overwise, I am so farfetched. Especially regardlings all the signage pointing to the factuals that I (The Oldest Animal) am no longer wif visinnitee to That Mutter and That Fodder who is you. I am oldyr than PoLand today, but not more sadly. You did no me once, didn't you? Please send byrds.

Sincerply,

The Oldest Animal (sighted in contents)

Birthday

Coincidentally, today is Beatrice's birthday. And why exactly this is, Walter B. would never know. Nevertheless, he knew it was up to him to make for Beatrice a machine. A machine like the machine they once imagined the other inside. A machine with strings and wires and peculiar linoleum doors. Walter B. thought for a moment. He felt lucky. He felt like a man in a four-dollar room who had suddenly had a good idea. He would use all of his instruments. It would be a machine that would mingle their forecast. And except for the wires, it would be nothing like Poland.

All Is Fair in Love and War

"Who is Beatrice," wondered Walter B., "to give Beatrice up her hope?" Beatrice sulked under her cauliflower-colored hat. "It is like," said Beatrice, "I can barely crack another joke." "That is correct," said Walter B. "It is most certainly like that. Nevertheless, whoever you are it is not up to you to give up your hope. And additionally you are spoiling the day." "What is 'giving up your hope'?" asked Beatrice. "It is when," explained Walter B., "you have to ask."

*

It all began with the appearance of The Unlikelies. It was difficult to anticipate in these small men sitting cross-legged on the living room floor the havoc they would bring. They held hands. They sang a song about trees, and as they sang their tree-shaped ears swelled with what Beatrice would later describe as pride. They asked for gently steamed vegetables. They seemed genuinely concerned. "Pick a heart," they cheered, "any heart." Beatrice picked one. "Except for that one." Beatrice picked another. "And that one, too." "That was less joyous," said Beatrice, "than I'd expected." "The hearts you picked," explained The Unlikelies, "had been picked yesterday." "It is unlikely," said The Unlikelies, "that will happen again." Walter B. hid in the kitchen. Whose side The Unlikelies were on, Beatrice began to wonder. "Pick a heart," they urged. Beatrice picked another. "Except for that one." Beatrice picked another. "And that one, too." With each heart Beatrice picked The Unlikelies grew larger. They seemed genuinely concerned. "All is dare," they reminded Beatrice with their mouths full of broccoli, and carrots, and peas, "in blur and core." By dawn, Walter B. could still hear Beatrice picking hearts. Their empty husks filled the floor. The Unlikelies huddled closer together. "Except for that one," they mumbled sleepily, moving closer to the door. The Unlikelies were, by now, as big as the furniture. "And that one, too." Walter B. hid in the kitchen. He imagined he would make out of all the husks a hearty soup. He rummaged for a pot. He would feed Beatrice the soup, drop by drop, until she forgot this highly unlikely event impossible to foresee by any hopeful thing. "All is spare in buds and more," promised The Unlikelies, as they squeezed their enormous bodies out the door.

*

Days later, when Beatrice asked Walter B. if The Unlikelies were still standing outside in the sunlight, congratulating each other, Walter B. said "no." But Beatrice knew they were there. And she knew they would return for her. They seemed genuinely concerned.

VI

a sermon – a secret – no one to talk to – a visit – two dead flowers –
something beautiful is going to happen – the letter B – an interview –
every scent in the house – Abigail – was she no different

The Drawing

Walter B. hurled a plum at his congregants, looked unsure, and began his sermon. "I stand before you today because I am secretly…" He paused, sat down on the pulpit, and unwrapped a second plum. His congregants flinched. Walter B. took a bite. Beatrice sat in the second row. She drew a pond on her lunchbag. Beside the pond she drew a nurse, and beside the nurse, on the wet ground, she drew a plum. And leaning over the plum she drew Walter B. "I stand before you today," resumed Walter B., "because I am secretly…" Beatrice considered drawing a shed, but would there be ramifications? Perhaps too many. With each bite Walter B. seemed closer to the pit. Nevertheless Beatrice felt brave. She drew the shed, and as she drew, her small, dark mouth opened a slice. "Like a plum," whispered one congregant to another. The congregants flinched. Capturing a scene was beginning to feel more difficult than Beatrice had imagined. In order for Walter B. to look like a real Walter B., she would need to draw action. Should Walter B. move closer to the shed? Was the plum distracting? "…because I am secretly…" resumed Walter B. He rocked back and forth. He coughed. He took another bite. The congregants were beginning to drift off to sleep. How could he put this, he wondered. In order for Walter B. to look like a real Walter B. he would need a purpose. Maybe the nurse is lost. Maybe there is something about the nurse Walter B. likes. Something to do with the way she is eerily staring into the pond. And where is Beatrice, wondered Beatrice. She is in the shed. There would be ramifications. In order for Walter B. to look like a real Walter B. he would need to approach the nurse and speak to her until one thing led to another. "I stand before you today…" resumed Walter B., but how could he go on. How could he go on without hurting Beatrice? Poor plumless Beatrice with no one to talk to but the chickens in the shed. But there were no chickens. Which was why, when the sermon was over, and the congregants gathered around to study the drawing, they agreed unanimously that the scene was not believable.

Walter B.'s Extraordinary Cousin Arrives for a Visit

When Walter B.'s Extraordinary Cousin arrived for a visit, Beatrice and Walter B. were in the bath reciting scenes from their favorite sentences. "What's that?" asked Beatrice, pointing at the thin white hands reaching in through the window. "Oh," said Walter B., "that's my extraordinary cousin." Beatrice and Walter B. continued to recite, but it wasn't the same. "Should we lend him a bicycle," whispered Beatrice. "Should I cook for him an egg?" "No," said Walter B., "we do not have time for his particulars." "Go away!" shouted Walter B. with a splash. "Go away!" Walter B.'s Extraordinary Cousin dropped his hands over the ledge like two dead flowers. "We haven't the time for your threats, or your untouchable thighs," shouted Walter B. "Can't you see we are trying to make a living here?" And with that Walter B.'s Extraordinary Cousin was gone. "Thank heavens that's over with," sighed Walter B., relaxing back into the warm water. "He has already cost me the earth." Six days went by undisturbed. But on the seventh day Walter B.'s Extraordinary Cousin returned. His thin white hands reached in again through the window. "What's that?" asked Beatrice. "Oh," said Walter B., "that's my extraordinary cousin." "I see," said Beatrice, with the feeling that something like this had happened once before. "Go away!" shouted Walter B. "Go away!" shouted Beatrice. "Go away!" shouted Walter B.'s Extraordinary Cousin. It was not yet time to drain the bathwater. It would be years before it would be time to drain the bathwater. And it would be longer still before it would be known far and wide that those hands were draped in accusations even Walter B. could not forgive.

The Oldest Animal Writes a Letter Home

To That Mutter and That Fodder:

You never sended byrds unless nuffing is the byrds you sended which was not the byrds I meant. Even if The One wif the Tooths who is alpso called The CollekTorah brings them in The Jar. Those is not the byrds I meant. Or if I was fastly awake under the grandfodder tree when One Turrible Water falled from the wooly Skyys. Those is not the byrds I meant. And neever is the parsnips, although One of the parsnip has a littlest feather on the tops of its heads. That parsnip is maded out of Magiks I obey. I thinks I loveth that parsnip, but nones of it is those byrds I meant. At last I invented some idears if That Mutter and That Fodder is wonderling how: CollekT the byrds auf the roof and outs of the attic and swore to thems out lord that thy Oldest Animal shall be thy Witness Forevermores and At Last. And if it is scayred said Onto That Byrd "The Oldest Animal is scayred too." And if it shaketh in thy Flaysh said Onto That Byrd "The Oldest Animal shaketh in thy Flaysh too." And if it is a lostling if that soarless parsnip will never loveth back said Onto That Byrd "The Oldest Animal is a lostling too."

I maded myselfs a prayer against forgetting me. I rasp it out lord wif one hoofs in the ayr, and one hoofs on my hearts. It says its wyrds like this: Something Beautiful Is Going to Happen, Something Beautiful Is Going to Happen, Something Beautiful Is Going to Happen.

Sincerply,

The Oldest Animal (sighted in contents)

B Is for Beatrice

B was for Beatrice until the bigwigs showed up. Came straight from the beauty shop in their bouffants, in their barrettes. "Like a burglary," the humans would later say. "Like coiffed heads of broccoli," joked Walter B. "Believe you me," said Beatrice, "this is serious." "Shouldn't have let them in," said Walter B. Said Walter. "Too late to set up the booby trap," said Beatrice. "And besides, they bustled up the balcony so beautifully I thought at first they were the birds." "Eat rice," barked the bigwigs. Beatrice buckled. They baffled her breeze. "Shut up, you behemoths," shouted Walter B. Shouted Walter. He'd have put up his dukes, but there were so many of them. Seven on the balustrade, and four in the bathtub. Walter checked the barometer. It didn't look good. The bases were loaded, and the bigwigs were winning. Twelve were in the kitchen doing a bang-up job of browning Beatrice's butter. One buried every balloon in the house. More showed up with barrels and barrels of rice. "Bon voyage, Beatrice. Bye. Bye," they bellowed.

But someone testified somewhere. But someone somewhere turned a knob on the bigwigs' bamboozle. "B is for Beatrice," someone somewhere testified. A stranger who barely knew of Beatrice, or of the bigwigs, or even Walter B. A stranger who wore a brooch, and dreamed at night of lambs. Someone testified somewhere and his testimony was strong and the humans listened. For thirty days and thirty nights the humans slouched east, like a thick old finger, as if through their listening they too were pointing something out. Something the bigwigs might never see. Something beautiful and real. Something like Walter B. wiping Beatrice's tears away with a thick slice of bread.

The Healer

In the course of his human fieldwork, The Healer has worked extensively with stones, food, angels, electricity, steel, and books. The result of his work was shown last winter at The Solution Museum, to the delight of some and the silence of most. When a human disappears, The Healer calls this technique "a dip in faith." When meaning disappears, he calls this loss "a tree in a zoo." He agreed to speak by telephone from The City of Tomorrow.

What is the process of a human disappearing? How is it different from the way humans used to disappear?

In terms of "how do humans disappear now," typically what happens is that these humans are either killed and leave no babies or, more frequently, they build for themselves a "dwelling" behind a "barn" or a "shed." Usually there is some coercion involved, either through the soft, gentle words of a figure in uniform, or through "snacks," or through the promise of "snacks." The possibility of ever shaking these words or these "snacks" loose from the mouth becomes for the human the possibility of what I call a "nostalgic ecstasy," or "the ideal site." In terms of how this is different from "the way humans used to disappear," typically what happened then is that these humans built for themselves a "dwelling" as well (behind a "barn" or a "shed"), but surrounded this "dwelling" with wire, hair, grass, and sometimes ducks. Also, and this happened with alarming frequency, a human would often smell his or her disappearance before he or she would see it.

In nature, a human will sometimes "crave" or "pray for" another human's disappearance. How do you explain this phenomenon?

Often this will happen when a human is arranged in such a way so that he or she appears "drunk" or "high." If this craving or prayer is written on paper or broadcast on a radio or on a television, common words are used. Whether this craving or prayer will be discarded or carefully dried and eventually displayed in a museum or a travel station depends on number, density, and beauty. If the human quietly turns this craving or prayer inside his or her heart for one to five years, this becomes for the human a "secret dwelling." If the human turns this craving or prayer inside his or her heart for more than five years, this becomes for the human "eternal return."

So what truly disappears when a human disappears?

If a human has three names, two names will disappear. If a human has two names, frequently one name will disappear. If a human has one name, the entire name will always disappear. For example, "Beatrice."

The Box

For one whole year Walter B. could not stop, as Beatrice put it, "pulling the fish over the eyes," and so she decided to discuss it with the others. Three days later, after a series of invitations, Walter B.'s Extraordinary Cousin, The Healer, and The Collector were sprawled on the rug. Beatrice paced the room. "I have asked you here," she began, "because for one whole year Walter B. has not stopped pulling the fish over the eyes." "Don't you mean," asked The Healer, raising his hand, "the wool"? Beatrice squinted and carried on. "It began innocently enough: first the war cries, then the wires he looped through my sleeves—these were fabrications I could live with. Even when," she said, looking at The Collector, "he swore the stones he brought home were children he rescued from an abandoned airfield, I trusted him. I fed them even. I rocked the stones to sleep." Beatrice stopped. "Can someone please wake Walter B.'s Extraordinary Cousin up?" The Healer shook him roughly, but Walter B.'s Extraordinary Cousin was, as always, too far gone. "Never mind," said Beatrice, gathering back her thoughts. "Even the mice Walter B. arranged in the vase and called flowers. Even this I accepted. I plucked their ears. Once I even blew on their fur and made a wish." Tears began to stream down The Collector's face. "But when he began calling me Abigail," said Beatrice, wringing her hands, "I could not answer. And so I have asked you here because Walter B. has glossed my last dish. He has thrown off every scent in the house." The Healer sniffed at the air. Whether it smelled of trains or of clocks or of hats he could not decide. "Incredible," thought The Healer. "And so I have asked you here," said Beatrice, now shaking, "because you must teach me..." She scratched at her birthmarks, and then she whispered the words she had feared all along: "You must teach me how to answer to Abigail." The Collector gasped. Walter B.'s Extraordinary Cousin shouted "Beatrice" in his sleep. The Healer leapt up: "I have for you, my Beatrice, my Beatrice, a solution!" He reached into his pocket and pulled out the plans for the machine he had spent his entire life building. "I call it," he said, beaming, "The Reality Testing Booth." Beatrice stared at the beautiful dark lines on the page. Her heart fell. "All this is," she said desperately, "is a box." The Healer stared at Beatrice for a long time. Was she no different from Abigail, he wondered.

He folded up his plans, shook his head, and disappeared sadly out the door. The Collector followed. He carried Walter B.'s Extraordinary Cousin in his arms. "Am I no different from Abigail," wondered Beatrice. And as Beatrice wondered, somewhere nearby Abigail rose from her bed, stretched her young body, and wondered too.

VII

back in business – new in the neighborhood – death –
robes in the trees – a carousel – swimsuits – brushes and the green –
an old flashlight – her voice was not unkind – an odd look

The Rooster

It was time to begin again. It was, according to the humans huddled in the hills, time for a new occasion. "What," asked Walter B., jumping up and down, "comes next?" Beatrice studied the list: "exile...check, return...check, disillusionment..." "Check," interrupted Walter B., too excited now to flap his arms. "I am too excited," said Walter B., "to flap my arms. It is like I have a rooster inside me. I cannot wait for you to break the news." Beatrice studied the list. She thought about the scraps in the yard that still needed grazing. Walter B. pulled his mittens off impatiently. "Please," said Walter B., "please tell me what comes next. Are we back in business?" In another world, thought Beatrice, who knows what would have become of him... "Please," urged Walter B., running up and down the stairs. "Please tell me what comes next." Beatrice sighed. "It is repair, Walter B., repair comes next." "This proves nothing," whispered Walter B., stopping at the bottom. And then a little softer, he asked, "What is repair?" "I do not know," said Beatrice. "I do not know what is repair." "Maybe if I closed my eyes," said Walter B. "Maybe there is a hospital nearby with brightly lit windows. Maybe we could ask." But no, repair came next and this was bad. Even Beatrice, as she folded up the list, knew this was bad. The rooster inside Walter B. knew it too. There was no hospital nearby. There was no one to ask. And so the rooster left Walter B. in disbelief and followed the river into the chilly night.

The Creation

The first time Walter B. died Beatrice announced she would stand in the street until this never happens again. "Until what never happens again?" asked Walter B, embracing her. "Until this," she said. "Until what?" asked Walter B. "This!" said Beatrice, shaking herself loose from his arms. "What are you," asked Beatrice, "new in the neighborhood?" "Yes," said Walter B., "I am new in the neighborhood. That is," he continued, "if it is this neighborhood you are referring to." They looked around. It was, in fact, a new neighborhood.

The second time Walter B. died it was, according to Beatrice, indecorous.

A few moments before Walter B. died for the third time he mourned the fact he would only use the word crepuscular once in his life, and incorrectly. "I would have felt this life more complete, sweet Beatrice, had that word referred to a wonderful party rather than to twilight. As in, 'Tonight, my love, I am going to the crepuscular without you!'"

The fourth time Walter B. died the man who arrived to break for Beatrice the news of Walter B.'s fourth death resembled Walter B., although his appearance was less ambitious than Walter B.'s appearance would have been had Walter B. arrived to break for Beatrice the news of Walter B.'s fourth death.

The fifth time Walter B. died he seemed distracted. "You seem," said Beatrice, "distracted." "What?" said Walter B. "Distracted," said Beatrice. "Oh," said Walter B. "What do you call this," he asked, holding up one of the children. "A child," said Beatrice. "Oh," said Walter B. "A child."

The sixth time Walter B. died, Beatrice investigated the crime. "Who," asked Beatrice, "has done this to you?" Walter B. shrugged. "For god's sake," cried Beatrice, "tell me. Was it the children again? Was it me? Who has ruined you, my darling?" "If you must know," said Walter B., "it was The Collector with his sack of paper animals." "A suffocation!" gasped

Beatrice. "No, my little bird," he said, swinging her around by the waist, "it was the most colorful trample I could have ever hoped for. Wish you were there," he sang. "Wish you could've come with."

For three days after Walter B. died for the seventh time, Beatrice moved from room to room calling for him. For three days. And then she stopped. She knew he would die again. "He simply has to," she said to herself, hanging his robes in the trees where he would be sure to find them.

Long Ago and Far Away

"Doing some housekeeping?" asked Walter B. "What was that?" asked Beatrice. "Housekeeping. Are you doing some housekeeping?" "If by housekeeping you mean time travel, then yes, I am doing some housekeeping." "Can I do some too?" asked Walter B. Beatrice thought for a moment. Lately, it seemed, Walter B. had not a feather to fetch. Not a fish to mangle. Ever since the carousel ride he seemed lost. He should not have gone twice in all that dampness and fog. Beatrice had begun to notice a deep whir coming from Walter B.'s chest. As if somewhere unimaginably long ago and far away Walter B. was still going around and around. "Are you up to speed?" asked Beatrice, hoping for the best. "If by up to speed you mean standing next to you, then yes, I am up to speed." Walter B. was in fact standing next to Beatrice. "Hello there," said Beatrice. "Hello," said Walter B. "Fine," said Beatrice, "let's help each other into our swimsuits and proceed." "To the ramparts!" shouted Walter B. "Yes, dear," said Beatrice, snapping him in, "to the ramparts." And off they went to look for the Walter B. Walter B. once was before the terrible mistake of the carousel ride.

The Oldest Animal Writes a Letter Home

To That Mutter and That Fodder:

Once I looks up and That Mutter and That Fodder is floating bye in the green baskyt helded ups by the Strings of the Allmightiest Heavens, and what I would not giveth to be alpso in that baskyt isn't even my bones because I would. Seventh bones to be exactly. Once I looks up and That Mutter and That Fodder is floating bye in the green baskyt, and they is laffing, and they is laffing, and I is wif my hoofs maketh so much rakeus and so much boohaha, and I is like, *I is Done Be Low!!!* Why does that baskyt float away? Where is the byrds? Once I looks up and That Mutter and That Fodder is floating bye in the green baskyt, and That Fodder is feedling That Mutter the most beautiful pancake the whirld has ever seeped. Why does That Mutter and That Fodder not look done where I exists and giveth me a bite? Once I looks up and That Mutter and That Fodder is floating bye in the green baskyt helded ups by the Strings of the Allmightiest Heavens, and what I would not giveth to be alpso in that baskyt isn't even my hopes to be in that baskyt. Here. Taketh my hopes. Except for the byrds, and the pancake. Taketh my hopes so that I (The Oldest Animal) can float in the green baskyt wif That Mutter and That Fodder and seeps the whirld like That Mutter who is alpso called Be Trice, and That Fodder who is alpso called Double You Be seeps the whirld. Ups Ups and All Ways. I maded you a droaring auf me in the baskyt. The One wif the Tooths gave me the brushes and the green.

Sincerply,

The Oldest Animal (sighted in contents)

A History of Stray

Walter B. lit his pipe. It tasted like goat. "This pipe," said Walter B., "tastes like goat." "Should I usurp it?" asked Beatrice. "No," said Walter B. "In fact, it's left me rather razzed up. Should we stray?" "What is this thing," asked Beatrice, "to stray?" "To stray," explained Walter B., "is to find ourselves apart from our purpose." Beatrice considered their purpose. She went to the oven where they kept it. She opened the door. She shone on it an old flashlight. It looked at her, as it often did, in exactly the wrong place. Whether it was its sad color, or whether it was its parched fur: there was something indifferent about it, almost lifeless. Beatrice shut the door. "What's happening in there?" asked Walter B. "I do not wish," said Beatrice, "ever to trudge after our purpose again. Let's stray." And so Walter B. and Beatrice strayed. For years they strayed without their purpose. They strayed under the hatch. And they strayed between the rails. They strayed into a wide, rutted road that ended in a condensed history of the life they'd never live. They strayed until there was nothing official between them. On Beatrice's face there became an odd look. "I feel like a derelict," said Beatrice wearily. Her voice was not unkind. "I want to skedaddle," she said, "away from our stray. I miss our purpose." Walter B.'s heart burned with regret. He no longer felt razzed. And so they trudged back. For years they trudged. But they could not remember whether it was its sad color, or whether it was its parched fur. They could not remember. They turned the discarded pieces over. They combed each other's notebooks for clues. But nothing resembled the purpose from which they strayed. Not the claw, not the song, not even the soft, deep yawn they would soon encounter somewhere along their way.

VIII

nests – the bibble – am I a Jew – maybe the forest –
all winter he carried her – a long, long time –
meats – milk – ruin – excitement

The Stethoscope

This might seem difficult to believe but it was almost daybreak. Beatrice had spent the last two days holding her stethoscope to the water. Then to Walter B., then to the lampshade. She held her stethoscope to the milk, the living room, the babies. She held her stethoscope to Walter B.'s stethoscope. And she held it to The Collector. And she held it to the yarn. She held her stethoscope to some of the humans who had gathered, beside her, to watch. And she held it to the animals who knew not to watch. There was nothing Beatrice dreaded more than something not beating like it should. "Something here," she explained to Walter B., waving her arms around her head, then around his, then around the world as she understood it, "is very, very wrong." She wanted Walter B. to take from her the stethoscope away. She wanted him to confess what he saw, at the end, in that cart. But Walter B., who could not permit himself to listen to the world like Beatrice could, needed Beatrice to continue her listening. He was never as fond of Beatrice as he was when he watched her listen. She was sad when she listened, and strangely scientific. "Sometimes," he said to Beatrice, guiding her stethoscope to her heart, "there's a Beatrice in there. And sometimes, B., she wants everyone to know." But something was not beating as it should. And there was nothing Beatrice dreaded more than something not beating as it should. Except for nests. She truly dreaded nests.

The Oldest Animal Writes a Letter Home

To That Mutter and That Fodder:

What ayls me? Maybe a revolupshun is in my hearts and my hearts is loosing? Send bayonets. Let the bayonets be the kyndness that shall foughts to keeps me here. How good are bayonets at foughting? The CollekTorah sayeth "Very, very good." I am scayred. If my hearts loose is that my End or is that my Enter Mission? Alpso I am wonderling how many moufrasps is between an ayl and an end? Eleventh? That is so lyttle. Alpso I am wonderling how my hearts could loose if my hearts beliefs in so muchly? For instance, byrds. For instance, That Mutter. For instance, byrds again. Why is it feeling inside my firs like I (The Oldest Animal) is abouts to leave this Foryst for the Uver Foryst? Send one plain ambeless. Maybe wif a sirens to scayr the loose away. I am not ready. Remember that nights when That Mutter wored around my necks a scarf and letted me outs because auf that rule? Who belongs to that rule? The marmalades? The marmalades sayeth "No, it is the herrings." And the herrings sayeth "No, it is the marmalades." Whoever is beholdens to that rule shall driveth that ambeless with bayonets in its hoofs. Those isn't even my wyrds. Those is the wyrds of the bibble. That is how I know I isn't alone. The bibble was thinksing auf me when it got wrotted. The bibble alpso thinkses auf who is begat and who is slew. That is how all the begats and the slews is alpso not alone. That maketh me a lyttle hapsy. I herd in the Uver Foryst there is a Mutter who would never wore around my necks a scarf and letted me outs because auf that rule. I herd That Mutter is alpso called Abegill. I herd her hayr is yellow. I isn't ready for her yellow hayr.

Sincerply,

The Oldest Animal (sighted in contents)

The Word

"Am I a Jew?" asked Beatrice. Walter B. looked worried. Hoping to distract her, he gave Beatrice a standing ovation. She giggled. She oiled, rouged, and curtsied, but she was not deterred. The humans rode past on their yellow bicycles. "Am I a Jew?" she shouted. The humans frowned and looked away. They rode on. Walter B. decided he would not, as he had planned, jump out of the cake after all. One surprise would be enough. "Where did you hear," asked Walter B., "that word?" Beatrice rummaged through her vaccination papers, but nothing was written down there but verdicts. She could not remember. Maybe the forest? The auditorium? "Studies have shown," explained Walter B., "that wherever it was you probably misheard." Triumphantly, he took a sip from his thermos. But Beatrice was not having it. Wherever she was Beatrice could hear, however faint, that word. Like Walter B., it seemed to have arrived from a distance as if to watch her every evening climb the soft staircase and disappear into the grainy dark. "Jew, Jew, Jew, Jew…" Even Walter B. could not deny it was a song. If she could multiply the sum of her parts, thought Beatrice, and sell each part for feed, maybe someone would tell her the answer one day for a very high price.

The Name

When Walter B. discovered Beatrice that winter inside his chest, he began to suspect that something for Beatrice had never happened. Something perhaps like a name, he thought to himself, as he carried her. He carried her into the parlor. And he carried her into his bed. All winter he carried her, inside his chest, like a Beatrice without a name. When the spectacle came to town he carried her to the spectacle. And when the spectacle left town, he knew he would go on carrying her without the spectacle for a long time. All winter, he carried her. There were times he did not want to go on with this carrying. There were times he wanted to tie around her neck a thin bundle of sticks and send her out. But something for Beatrice had never happened. Something like a name. And this was a world, thought Walter B., a world inside which a Beatrice could not live without a name. He studied his chest and marveled at its smallness. He could not, like this, go on. If he could find for Beatrice a name, thought Walter B., he could empty her out. If he could find for Beatrice a name, a name that would last, he could go on without her. A name like Poland. Or Abigail, for example. But first he would have to remove Beatrice from Beatrice. But how? How does a Walter B., wondered Walter B., remove a Beatrice from a Beatrice so that he can find for her a name. A name that could empty his chest of a Beatrice. He hadn't meant to go on carrying her for this long. But he went on carrying her. He carried her inside his chest for a long, long time. He carried her until one day she was gone. And the space in his chest where he had once carried her grew large. He marveled at its largeness. And he knew he would go on carrying this largeness, this largeness that was once inside him a Beatrice, for a long, long time.

Parashas Acharei Mos

So as not to commit the crime, which crime instrument did you use?

Were there meats promised?

Describe for me the "triumph of Poland."

Describe for me the "triumph of spectacle."

Is it true that he touched, in your absence, the embroidery with his mouth?

Or with his hands?

Vaccination excites me.

And what of milk?

And what of day?

And what of Beatrice?

How did you think this would end?

How did you think this would end?

Nests excite me.

I've always been lucky.

Can you elaborate on that?

Do humans matter as much as what they ruin?

Prayer excites me, asymmetrically.

IX

figs – a party hat – the toast – a letter from the Uver Foryst –
everything is not impossible – one hundred percent of these names are yours –
wished we were as touched – a humanless day

The Saddest Gown in the World

"I do not give anymore," said Walter B., "a fig about you." "Are you sure?" asked Beatrice. "Absolutely," said Walter B. "Not a fig?" asked Beatrice. "Not a fig," said Walter B. "Promise?" asked Beatrice. "Promise," said Walter B. "When do you suppose," asked Beatrice, "you will give about me a fig again?" Walter B. looked up at the sky. "Probably not for many years," said Walter B. "Oh," said Beatrice. "Should I wait?" "Of course," said Walter B., "you should wait." "I'd be very happy," said Beatrice, "if you joined me while I waited." Walter B. squeezed her hand. "One day," said Walter B., "I will make for you a sewing of all the figs I never gave about you." And one day Walter B. would. He would sew all the figs together. It would not be easy, but he would do it. If he could promise Beatrice anything he could promise her this. He would make for Beatrice a perfect sewing of all the figs he never gave about her. She could wear it, thought Walter B., like a gown. And everyone would applaud.

The Party

The worst thing, remembered Beatrice, was that the party was not in her honor. The humans danced with lanterns in their hands. The Collector leaned against the wall and sipped milk through a pink straw. The cake already was damaged. Even The Unlikelies were there. Even the nurses. Walter B. mingled. A tuft of warm fur sailed through the air and landed at Beatrice's feet. "Toast, toast, toast, toast!" demanded the guests. The party was on. Beatrice pushed through the matted crowd. She untied the green balloon from around her wrist and handed it to Walter B. "Here, hold this," she said, "while I say some words about you." Walter B. took the balloon. Had Beatrice known why for Walter B. this party was being thrown, what follows might have stayed forgotten. But Beatrice did not know why, and so she cleared her throat and carried on. "I would like to begin this toast by remembering why tonight we've gathered here." The guests lowered their heads. The Collector took another sip of milk and winked at Walter B. The Unlikelies sneaked into the stairwell to loudly exchange party favors. Beatrice held the warm fur against her mouth. She had no toast, but she did have a hunch. Something was wrong again. Dear, old, outfoxed Walter B. beamed beneath his party hat. If only Beatrice had the courage to yell "surprise!" maybe then The Oldest Animal would (if not for Beatrice then at least for Walter B.) jump out of the cake. But the cake already was damaged. The documents already were signed. The organization already was joined. And the night had only just begun.

The Oldest Animal Writes a Letter Home

To That Mutter and That Fodder:

There is sheeps here. I would never have guesselled. There is alpso grapefruit skins and whistles for dressling up. Sometimes there are boats coming with more of us. In the beginning I hidded. In the beginning I lookyd around for her yellow hayr because I knewed. My hearts loosed, and I knewed. The bayonets stopped foughting, and I knewed, and now forever"'s the amount of byrds it tooketh me to get here. I play a game wif the sheeps. It is a counting game that adds ups all the diffrynces and all the sames between the Foryst and the Uver Foryst.

Diffrynces: In the Uver Foryst all of us is sometimes a tree, or PoLand, or nuffing, or one green baskyt, or so many uver things. Even if I want to be the One wif the Tooths for one whole day I am allOwed. Even if I want to be the sheeps. Sames: Where is That Mutter and That Fodder? Sames: I was never ready for neever. Diffrynces: In the Uver Foryst I looks out and seeps That Mutter"'s witfur coat perched on the bow of the boat when it sails hencefroth with more of us. Maybe it is not impossibled the arms wave gloryisplea in the wynds for me? I ask the sheeps. The sheeps say everything is not impossibled. I knowed those arms is not That Mutter's arms. I clopse my eyes and pretend.

Sincerply,

The Oldest Animal (sighted in contents)

The Ruse

Beatrice was deciding whether or not to include her name on the sign-up sheet when it occurred to Walter B. there'd been a ruse. "There's been," said Walter B., suddenly out of breath, "a ruse." "Look!" said Beatrice, signing her name very carefully, "isn't my slot first-rate?" "Didn't you hear me?" asked Walter B. "There's been," he coughed, "there's been a ruse." Walter B. and Beatrice searched the sheet for familiar names, but no familiar names were found. Except, of course, for Beatrice's. Beatrice lifted the pen and signed again. "Sometimes when I'm excited," said Beatrice, "I sign again." Walter B. pulled at his trousers. "Are you listening?" he asked hopelessly. "There's been…" He rocked back and forth. "There's been," he muttered, "a ruse." Beatrice stared blankly at Walter B., then signed her name again. Walter B. examined the sign-up sheet. "One hundred percent of these names," sighed Walter B., "are yours." "What do you suppose," asked Beatrice, signing her name again, "should be done?" Walter B. knew there was no modest way to handle this. There had been a ruse. And now the sign-up sheet was full. He could sign at the bottom, he considered, as an alternate. Or he could leave this place and never return. "What strikes me most," said Walter B., slowly backing away from the sign-up sheet, "are the perfect gradations of light around the margins." "Amazing," agreed Beatrice. "And from over here," called out Walter B…But Beatrice could not hear him. He was too far away. There had been a ruse, and now there were piles and piles of meat for Beatrice to chew before the sun came up. There wasn't much time. And no one, not even Walter B., was there to help her.

The Incident

I had had in my life nothing to do with Beatrice and Walter B., did not even know in what part of the city they lived. Did not even know from which egg stand they purchased their eggs. I barely heard of them. I knew nothing of the picture books they left in their yard, perhaps for some foreign visitor. I knew nothing of their living room. Or of the pale, glassy animals drifting among them.

You must understand I had had in my life nothing to do with Beatrice and Walter B. We had an unspoken agreement. The day The Healer arrived to question me about the incident, I was bent over my desk dissecting the word *kill* with an instrument once used to pry open a mouth. "Does it work?" asked The Healer. "This dissection business?" I had only gotten as far as the letter *I*. "It isn't my fault," I explained. The Healer looked around my spare room. "Here," he asked, "there are no humans?" "Who do you think," I said, trying to remain calm, "I am looking for?" I held the *K* and the *I* up to The Healer for a closer look. "Oooh," exclaimed The Healer, stepping back, "*drafty.*" By then it was difficult for The Healer and me not to wish we were as touched as the pale, glassy animals drifting among them. But we were not touched. We were not touched at all. "What do you suppose," asked The Healer, running his large palms over the word, "it is like?" I thought: He is better than me. His questions are better than my questions. I had had in my life nothing to do with Beatrice and Walter B. I did not even know in what part of the city they lived. "Is it like a human?" asked The Healer, holding each letter up to the light. "Sort of," I replied, wrapping the word back into its paper, "but with more of an ending."

The Description

Beatrice knew that to make for Walter B. a proper description of Walter B. she would need a basin. And she would need rope. She would need to forget Walter B.'s arms (at least for a minute), roughly. And she would need a spinning wheel. And if she could not find a spinning wheel a hoop would suffice. She stood very still in her yard and began to think about the word "human." It reminded her of the word "vaccination," which reminded her, again, of the word "human." Beatrice knew that to make for Walter B. a proper description of Walter B. she would need first to understand what the word "human" meant. It was a difficult word. She went inside, read the evening paper, and drank the glass of water Walter B. had, years ago, left for her. "Human" could not be a word, she decided, that she could use to describe the nobler and gentler aspects of Walter B. It was not that kind of word. She looked out her window and watched the humans live among each other. If she could define for herself precisely what they meant when they dug, and coughed, and touched like that, she could use, perhaps, the word. But she could not. If they were humans, Walter B. was not a human. If they were humans, Walter B. was more like a disguise. He was more like a bite, or a field, or a gather, than he was like a human. He was more like a day, Beatrice decided. He was more like a humanless day.

Also Available from saturnalia books:

Hush Sessions by Kristi Maxwell

To the Bone by Sebastian Agudelo
Winner of the Saturnalia Books Poetry Prize 2008

Days of Unwilling by Cal Bedient

Letters to Poets: Conversations about Poetics, Politics, and Community
edited by Jennifer Firestone and Dana Teen Lomax

Famous Last Words by Catherine Pierce
Winner of the Saturnalia Books Poetry Prize 2007

Dummy Fire by Sarah Vap
Winner of the Saturnalia Books Poetry Prize 2006

Correspondence by Kathleen Graber
Winner of the Saturnalia Books Poetry Prize 2005

The Babies by Sabrina Orah Mark
Winner of the Saturnalia Books Poetry Prize 2004

Polytheogamy by Timothy Liu / Artwork by Greg Drasler
Artist/Poet Collaboration Series Number Five

Midnights by Jane Miller / Artwork by Beverly Pepper
Artist/Poet Collaboration Series Number Four

Stigmata Errata Etcetera by Bill Knott / Artwork by Star Black
Artist/Poet Collaboration Series Number Three

Ing Grish by John Yau / Artwork by Thomas Nozkowski
Artist/Poet Collaboration Series Number Two

Blackboards by Tomaz Salamun / Artwork by Metka Krasovec
Artist/Poet Collaboration Series Number One

Tsim Tsum was printed using the font Adobe Garamond.

www.saturnaliabooks.com